The Three Wishes

Written and illustrated by

DAVID MELLING

Hodder
Children's
Books

A division of Hachette Children's Books

The King and Queen were away for a few days and the knight and his horse were appointed royal babysitters for the weekend. No problem, they thought.

But they soon decided
that babysitting wasn't
quite so easy.

And there was **SO**
much to tidy up!

'I would rather fly out of this window into a night of surprises than babysit tomorrow!' sighed the knight.

'Neigh!' snorted the horse, which meant, 'Be careful what you wish for, because if you believe in magic, anything can happen.'

Sure enough, within moments the knight and his horse tripped and slipped and crashed through the window, flying out into a night full of surprises.

'NOOOoooooooooooooooooooooooooooooooooooo!'

They landed in a tangled heap of arms and legs
on top of a little old lady and her donkey.

'Oh dear, I've spilt my bag of spells,' she gasped.
'Hurry! If you help me catch them I shall grant you
three wishes.'

The knight and his horse chased and
scrambled and caught the spells one
by one. It wasn't easy.

Finally, they were sure all the spells had been collected.
The old lady thanked them for their trouble and then,

with a 'poof' and a pink puff of smoke, she was gone.
But there was magic in the air.

And, oh dear, there was still one loose spell – a really, really naughty one.

The spell teased the knight, weaving its magic into his hair. The knight could only watch as the magic sprouted and grew!

'Eeek! We have three wishes!' flapped the knight.
'Quick, use one of them now.' So the faithful horse closed
his eyes and wished as hard as he could.

'**Aargh!** Our first wish is wasted!' wailed the knight. 'I don't like carrots and those fluffy slippers look ridiculous. I wish you hadn't done that – **oops!**'

'**Neigh! Neigh! Snort!** There goes the second wish!' whinnied the horse.

The knight and his horse were very cross with
each other for wasting two whole wishes. They just
wanted everything back the way it was before.
Eventually, they agreed to make the third wish
together.

Unfortunately, they each wished for different things –

and everything got mixed up!

'What are we going to do now?' said the knight.

'Neigh!' said the horse, which meant, 'Sit still, I have an idea.'

He took a pair of shears and set to work.

At last, they tidied themselves up, but stopped
suddenly when they heard something make
a funny noise.
'Oh no, now what?' groaned the knight.
'We've used up all our wishes.'

The knight panicked, so the horse panicked,
and they tried to run away.

But the naughty spell's magic was **still** growing and it snagged itself on the edge of the page. The **something** was getting closer.

It was the prince and princess.

They had come to find out who had made so much noise and woken them up!

'What's this?' they asked and pulled out the spell by its roots.

'Ouch!' said the knight.

Then the royal children led the knight and his faithful
horse safely back to their room.

The next day the naughty spell had gone and the prince and princess helped tidy up the castle... inside and out. To their surprise, the knight and his horse found themselves wishing they could babysit the prince and princess again.

Which just goes to show,
sometimes you don't need magic

to make your wishes come true.

Well, maybe sometimes.